DOWN MEMORY LANE

Roger Searing's

DOWN MEMORY LANE

Reading Between the Wars

Reading Chronicle/Countryside Books

First published 1985
©Reading Chronicle 1985

Countryside Books
3 Catherine Road
Newbury, Berkshire

ISBN 0 905392 56 6

Produced through MRM (Print Consultants) Ltd., Reading
Designed and typeset by Publicity Plus, Newbury
Printed in England by The Wembley Press Ltd, Reading

CONTENTS

ACKNOWLEDGEMENTS

The publishers are most grateful to the following people who kindly loaned their photographs. Their illustrations have done much to enhance the book:

Mrs A.N. Ambrose
Mr & Mrs S.A. Bowles
Mr A.R. Colyer
Mrs I. Harper
Mr R. Higgs
Mrs V. Kearey
Mrs C.M. Page
Mr E.G. Rolfe
Mr J. Stimpson
Mr E.J. Taylor
Mr E.T.G. Thatcher
Mrs Truss
Mr H.E. White
Reading Museum & Art Gallery

Introduction

A winter or two ago, during a bitterly cold spell of weather when the snow had been lying on the ground for several days, I amused myself by writing down the names I could remember of the shops which were in Reading's Broad Street in the 1920s. I cannot recall what prompted me to do it, and I do not recollect any purpose in doing it. I was surprised at the clear mental picture I had of this shopping area 60 years ago and the length of the list of shops I produced. I passed the list to my wife for comments and so followed pleasant hours of reminiscences, remembering more details of Broad Street as it was in our childhood and during the decades after the Great War. I rewrote the list, locating the shops and describing their merchandise and that was the first extract for the *Down Memory Lane* series which appeared in the *Midweek Chronicle*. And so I continued remembering.

The immediate response to these articles was remarkable. Readers of the *Midweek Chronicle* will know that letters poured in expressing pleasure at taking part in the journey down memory lane, adding to the memories, correcting some of the mistakes of my memory and providing details of our recollections. Tales of times and explanations solved some of the perplexities of the past. As I explained originally, the articles were based on my memories and at no time did I carry out any research on the subject of Reading between the Wars. I was happy with my memories and I did not want them dispelled. In this book, I have used some of the material contained in the letters published in the *Midweek Chronicle* to augment my original articles. Apart from the published letters, I have received many personal letters and phone calls from others who wished to join in the pleasant pastime of recalling childhood memories of our activites and the locations of them in the town of Reading between the Wars. How interesting it has been to have renewed contacts with many of those with whom I went to school up to 65 years ago, with those near whom I lived and whom I met many years ago! All of these reunions have yielded memories and I have tried to incorporate these in this book. (I have a long list in the back of my diary of the names and addresses of old friends I have yet to visit.)

It has been interesting to note that in spite of all the material advantages of living in the present time, most of us recall our childhood during the difficult times of the 20s with pleasure, and there has been a tendency to think of the good old days when we all know that our elders had many troubles. Youth is a time of fun and enchantment when all our days are sunny and all around is bright and beautiful. Or is it only in retrospect? Perhaps we have looked back and seen flowers blooming in the winter and sunshine through the clouds and rain. However, how enjoyable it has been to go back down memory lane and visit all of the corners of Reading, and remember all of the joys of living in this town at the time when our joints did not creak, when our hair flew in the wind, our eyes darted from one new sight to another and we were energetic. Reading was a splendid, attractive and exciting town to us. Thank you, Reading, for providing an excellent background for a growing boy. It was a wonderful time!

To any young readers I would say savour your youthful days in your home town, for what you experience now will provide the stuff that dreams are made of in your old age. My best wishes to you. I hope that one day you too will look back down memory lane with satisfaction. To the older generation I say thank you for your company in our travels into the past. May there be many more happy memories.

Roger Searing

The author as a small boy in the 1920s. His mother was still patriotically celebrating victory in the Great War with her choice of hat. The leggings were a forerunner of Wellington boots. In the twenties every infants' school teacher needed a button hook among her essential items for the classroom.

Shopping with Mum

It must have been my mother's favourite pastime, going shopping in or keeping an eye on Broad Street. When young, I was quite well informed about the shops in the centre of Reading and about those on the way to town. I suppose that before writing of my memories of these times, I should have researched it a little, but I prefer to rely upon memory; it would be a shame to destroy what I can remember so clearly! We would go into McIlroy's in Oxford Street on nearly every visit. Into Hedgecock's often, because my mother had been an apprentice milliner there and it recalled her youthful days.

We sometimes shopped in Bull's, rarely in Wellsteeds and never in Heelas'; that was where Queen Mary shopped and the one-armed commissionaire in a grey uniform gave the impression that this shop was not for us. It was many years later that I entered Heelas', even after the time I awaited outside for my girl friend who earned 2/1d per week as an apprentice there. These were the drapery stores. All of them had shop-walkers; over-dressed, haughty, suave fawning gentlemen who directed customers to the chair by the right counter. I enjoyed McIlroy's most; it was an enormous building stretching

Looking west along Broad Street. Minster Street is off to the left in this scene taken some 60 years ago. Just past the turning is Wellsteeds store.

from Cheapside nearly to West Street, but somehow there was not much inside. As in most stores at the time, much of the building was taken up by the living-in accommodation for the staff. I liked the basement and that long slope, made for running up and down, which led to 'materials' displayed in an area like the Natural History Museum in London.

Hedgecocks was not even moving with the times in the twenties. For my entertainment, Hedgecocks had (as a few other shops had too,) the extraordinary overhead railway system of sending money and sales sheet to the distant cashier, from whom the change and receipt would return in the small cylinder. How I would have liked to have pulled the handle on the end of a short rope which somehow started the propulsion to the distant spot! How did all those little cylinders get to the many points throughout the shop? Who changed the points? Bulls was next to Hedgecocks, but much larger and progressive. Strange that it eventually disappeared. But Wellsteeds was exciting; it had a restaurant circling the first floor, from which strains of 'In a Persian Market' carried to the

shoppers below. McIlroys, which Reading folk had difficulty in pronouncing and invented several forms of, was generally called 'Macs'. And then for me there was 'Awmack's' which prompted me to try to establish the relationship between these two establishments. Of course, there was none. Awmacks in Broad Street (opposite where Woolworths is now) sold a variety of simple arty crafty items.

I first recall Marks & Spencer as an open fronted shop - walk in and inspect the counters around the edge! The items were all very cheap - a real hotch potch - and I believe we referred to this shop opposite Wellsteeds (now Debenhams) as a bazaar. The toys were interesting, especially the mechanical ones, but these were taboo as most of them were stamped 'Made in Germany'. Suddenly, Marks & Spencer moved to the Oxford Street and West Street corner, on each side of the Maypole shop. It was a ground floor and basement shop and their image changed. Now they were a different kind of shop and I can remember gazing wondrously at a fine display of Christmas decorations - somewhere about 1924 I should think. I can remember the excitement of

13

Woolworths opening - a vast shop for those times and nothing for sale over 6d. I remember too, boys sorting through the debris as it was brought out to carts after a fire had reduced Woolworths stock to heaps of charred rubbish.

Broad Street was our main objective most days, but we did sometimes go into the Butts, reached by a short bottle-neck at the corner of which was Baylis', the grocers, a splendid shop, and I was quite in awe of the service provided. There was an annexe to Baylis' around the corner in Broad Street, the Huntley & Palmers biscuits shop. We bought our broken biscuits there, semi-sweet, sweet or best of all broken wafers. The man who served there was tall, stooped a little, bald, had a shiny rosy face, spoke in a quiet clear voice and wore a clean white coat and apron. Today I can see him clearly after sixty years, but I cannot remember anyone in the supermarket I used yesterday.

The Market and the Covered Market (The Arcade) were sources of bargains. The Arcade housed trestle-tabled 'shops'; hygiene was not held to be important, but at least the dusty pavement was frequently watered to keep dust from the unprotected food. Here, and at many other parts of Reading, was Eighteens the fishmongers - everyone knew the Eighteens and I always understood that Mrs. Dyer, the baby farmer and murderess, was apprehended because of the Eighteens' fish basket. There was another stall in the open market and here Eighteens sold off their fish during the Saturday evening at give away prices - a large haddock with herrings and bloaters thrown in, went for less than a shilling. The lighting flares looked most dangerous, hissing under the canopies. The cockle stall did good business and my weekly twopence often went on a quarter of a pound of mixed boiled sweets - loose on the table, piles of raspberry drops, red striped clove flavoured ones, pineapple drops, pink and white mint ones and a number of others whose flavour I liked but was not able to identify. We bought oranges very cheaply and also carried home the wood from orange boxes for kindling wood once or twice a year. Usually, for a birthday treat, we would have refreshment in the Talbot Cafe (over the shops on the corner of Queen Victoria Street and Broad Street). What a treat! A milky coffee and a H & P

Oxford Street as it was about 80 years ago. On the left is Langstons the outfitters and other shops where the Butts Centre now stands, while opposite was McIlroys Department Store.

chocolate wafer. Wonderful! Another treat, a little more frequent, was a small ½d cottage loaf from Tibbles the bakers (on the corner of Alfred Street) for my tea. I remember my first visit to the Vaudeville Cinema - Rudolph Valentino in 'The Sheik'. I was impressed later much more by Jackie Coogan, and my real favourite was Buster Keaton. However, treats did not come often. We were more likely to look in at Jacksons & Langstons, where boys like me could be clothed cheaply. Poynders was a favourite shop of my mother; she belonged to their library and we enjoyed looking at their fancy goods. Gasgoines, the Pork Butchers (nearly on the corner of The Butts and Oxford Street) had an attractive smell all of its own and I viewed the shop with some esteem because of the clean and attractive lay-out of their window. Collingwoods the Grocer was also an impressive and active shop, a few doors away and in between was Watts the Cycle Shop, with its stock merely for my admiration from outside.

Cullimores owned a shop in Southampton Street which sold faggots and peas. It was from here that many poor children of Reading obtained their best meal of the week. Even so, they chanted this uncomplimentary rhyme.

I went into old Cullimore's shop,
The stink was enough to blind me,
I looked at the faggots and they looked at me,
And the peas walked out behind me.

Sometimes we shopped close to home. There was Mr. Brewer's the butcher with his ice-chest and brine-tub under the counter. Miss Matthews sold us cottons and ribbons and Miss Onyett sweets and ice-creams from the shop where Mr. Onyett prepared his milk round. At the Co-op I marvelled at the butter-patting, the cheese cutting with a wire and all the hand made bags from a sheet of paper for sweets, sugar, tea, sultanas and so on. All these shops were within five minutes of the Battle Hospital.

Happy memories, yes! But there was much poverty and for many, shops were for looking at. The children who stood outside the Co-op cake shop (near Connaught Road) on cold winter's evenings around 8 p.m. were quiet and tense, desperately hoping that there would be a few unsold cakes at give away prices. Pleasure was very cheap, but still too dear for many.

What wonderful memories of shops and shopping in the twenties have been evoked by my original article. It was Mr. Love in the Huntley & Palmers biscuit department of Baylis' and it was Sid on the bacon slicing machine. I wonder if either of them expected to be recorded in the town's history? We took a jug to buy milk at the Creamery next to the Mitre (nearly gone) in West Street. Fortescue's, the cycle shop, had a penny farthing suspended above the shop and we boys gazed into the window to see and eventually to copy the latest working Meccano model. Awmacks in Broad Street had a railway line at the side of the shop for the quick delivery and despatch of goods. Seven or eight banana barrows did business around the town centre - very ripe bananas, two a penny. Next to the Vaudeville Cinema, a man sold 'Grandma's Chest Tablets' from a truck in a pub yard. And where were those coffee stalls frequented by tram crews,

early workers, drivers of horse vehicles etc? I am reminded - Cemetery Junction, the Butts, Berkeley Avenue, Grovelands Road, Radford Road, Caversham Bridge, the Railway Station, Valpy Street and St. John's Road, all conveniently located near loos and horse troughs. Cafes were very few - we hadn't the cash for such luxuries! Mrs. Elsie South, whose father owned Foote's Stores near the railway bridge in Oxford Road, reminded me of the activities of a family grocer in the 1920s. In this grocery business there were assistants, apprentices, and errand boys working from 8.00 a.m. until 7.00 p.m. (half day Wednesdays) and until 8.00 p.m. on Fridays and 9.00 p.m. on Saturdays. The writing out of customers' orders was a big task, and so was the weighing up of everything from large sacks, barrels, boxes and chests, using brass weights (always kept gleaming). Any customer who had forgotten the odd ½lb. butter or ¼lb. of tea would expect special delivery at any time on any day. There was also the task of covering the floor with damp saw-dust in order to reduce the dust rising from the wooden floors. Not surprisingly Mrs. South does not think too highly of the service given in shops today.

Cosilda Starkey has reminded me of the statement about Reading, 'Eighteen vicars at Death's Door!' At some time, Vicars, the newcomers to West Street, were told that in Reading now there were Eighteen Vicars at Death's door. When the first shock had passed it was explained that Eighteens were the fish-mongers, Vicars (the butchers) at Death's (the baker's) door.

It is said that Charlie Eighteen the fishmonger once took on an apprentice who was very keen to please. On the first day at work, the lad was told to wash the slabs. He was back quickly - 'Done that Mr. Eighteen,' he said. Next Charlie told him to go and arrange the watercress decoration. Again the apprentice was quick - 'Done that Mr. Eighteen.' He was told to put clean sawdust on the shop floor and once more returned quickly, 'Done that Mr. Eighteen,' he said. Exasperated, Charlie, who to say the least was a big man, told the lad to go and hang his back-side out of the window. Again the apprentice returned quickly, 'Done that Mr. Eighteen'. 'What did the people say?' asked Charlie. 'Good Morning Mr. Eighteen', the boy told him.

(From a letter from T.J. Simmonds of Woodley published in 'Midweek' on February 14th 1984.)

A number of my correspondents, including Mrs. Bernard from Adelaide in Australia, have memories of the lovely smells of Reading in the twenties. The Co-op bakery in Grovelands Road received many compliments for its wonderful aroma of newly baked bread and also praised were the many horse drawn baker's vans racing home along the Oxford Road late in the afternoon; they too had the crusty cottage loaf smell about them.

As I think of Reading smells, I remember Dunlops at the corner of Oxford Road and Howard Street, having a rich smell of meal, chicken and animal provender. Simmonds' Brewery certainly had its own 'hoppy' smell, but it was different across the road, where the coopers making the beer barrels produced a smell of wood carvers and blacksmiths working together. The most pungent smells were those from the tanneries in Katesgrove Lane. The Market Place had smells of all kinds, but the over-riding smell

Oxford Road, looking east. Miss Matthews' drapery shop is near the centre of the picture on the right hand side. The large building on the left is Elm Park Hall.

A group of workers at Burberry's factory.

was of squashed oranges at one end (by the stalls of Jock Messias and his sons, Ben, Lew and John) and fish and the cockle stall at the other, both gaining a touch of naptha from the evening flares. Pork butchers were particularly attractive to me. I suppose it was the strong, spicy smell they had. They were Gasgoine's in Oxford Street and Louis Rogers' in Friar Street and biggest of all, Venners' in Southampton Street where pigs were killed at the rear of the shop which had both a retail and wholesale trade. I was taken there as a small boy in a school party. I witnessed a blonde giant despatching squealing pigs then followed their carcases down a line of workers and eventually to a sausage making machine. My young friend was sure that the sausages were still moving! Pigs were also kept in the rear of Abery's shop in London Street. In about 1925, Mr. Abery asked me to take a bowl of lard to Mr. Meaby the baker in Queens Road and later the same day to collect lard cakes. Never has there been a 'lardy' such as I tasted that day; the aroma was just too tempting!

What other smells? The less said about Union Street (Smelly Alley, I am reminded) the better.

The pubs emitted a stronger smell than they do today. It must have been assisted by the sawdust covered floors. Let's finish with coffee and remember the fragrant haze coming from the Cadena Cafe in Broad Street.

Many of you have written of your experiences in the twenties as apprentices. Clearly, that is how the majority of us started our working lives. The drapery stores and others too must have staffed themselves mainly with lowly paid apprentices. Many of you say that at the end of your apprenticeship, three years or so, you were replaced by a new apprentice and that you looked around for another job to earn £1 per week. On the other hand, many of you have expressed appreciation of the skills you gained from an expert craftsman or tradesman; several of you rue the day this system of training virtually ended.

I was also reminded of the proper title of the department at Hedgecocks in Broad Street - the Mantle & Millinery Department, and in the workshop, there was a fine set of tools to make the wire frames to produce hats in the mode of Queen Mary.

Without radio or television to inform, I

suppose that it is not surprising that we children regarded those little cylinders travelling along the overhead wires to the cashier as a new wonder of the world. It was certainly intriguing to see these speeding from all corners of the shop to the cash desk and back again without error. I have been told that these cylinders did not always contain cash or receipts. Notes passed between members of the staff in these containers. Naughty teenagers of the twenties!

Looking along any side street in Reading in the twenties, particularly in winter, smoke from coal fires could be seen billowing from at least one chimney in every house. Factories belched smoke and so did the engines congregating in the maze of railway lines west of Reading station and near Coley. This smoke coupled with the moisture in the air from the river valleys encouraged fogs. *Real* fogs! Pea-soupers, similar to those experienced in London. I can remember feeling my way home along the railings and feeling lost in the middle of the road because I could see nothing on which to fix the direction I had come from and where I had to go to. I believed the poem which read, 'Tonight the fog hides stars on high, Ghosts, hobgoblins and witches fly'. One foggy night a neighbour wished to take his dog to the vets (in 1926, I believe) but could not find the wide entrance in Friar Street to Males the veterinary surgeon because of the dense fog.

We tend to look back with nostalgia, remembering the happy times, but not everything was bliss. To some extent, it was the suvival of the fittest and what were then killer diseases had yet to be conquered. Unemployment was rife and for those without work, life was grim, many experiencing dire poverty. Conditions at work for many were hard and comforts and pleasures rare. Most of us who were young in the twenties have had the good fortune to live in a period of opportunity and improvement. We appreciate our good fortune at the present time all the more for our experiences in the twenties.

Broad Street, looking east, photographed in the late 1920s. Baylis the grocer's shop is on the right.

Whiteknights long before it became the campus of Reading University. This view looks south towards Shinfield Road. It was the place to go on a winter's day such as this, to skate or slide on the lake.

Playing in the Park

'Where are you going?' 'Up the Park' would be my answer. And up it was; up one of the hill streets, but reached fleet of foot. It was crawling downhill, tired, hungry and thirsty on the homeward journey that always seemed a long way to me as a child. Palmer Park was splendid but reserved for high days and holidays when it hosted a fair, a fete or a show. It was flatter and there were few private corners and in any case, Prospect Park was nearer. I doubt if I ever expressed in my young days any affection for the Park - quite unknowingly I loved it and spent much time there. Our own garden was small and I would soon get giddy running around it; so up the Park I would go. The Park has not really changed since the twenties. It's all very much under control now; no part is wild and natural as it used to be, but I can easily locate the sites of my childish adventures, and the grass and the wind feel just the same.

I was told that my first encounter with the Park was in my pram and there I exchanged 'Goos' with a young fellow who has been my life long friend. Around the tennis courts was a social centre for West Reading, especially on a summer's evening. Gathered there were mothers and babies, lonely war widows, a few ancients, groups of subdued teenagers and children playing roly poly down the adjacent slopes, all of them watching infrequently the pat ball tennis played by stolid married couples. All in white, of course; it was too expensive for youngsters, a court was 1/- per hour! When I was big enough to run about, play ball and go roly-polying with the others, gnats took a particular liking to me and I would spend several days with my ears encased in dried starch and water.

It was not long before I escaped from maternal ties and explored the vastness alone. At first I ran and ran, dodging around the trees and in time, finding seclusion, lying down and gazing at the scudding clouds from a hide-away in the long grass. Yes - the long grass; after the football season, the grass was left undisturbed until June, haymaking time. Then my little friends and I would throw armfuls of hay at each other, make heaps for jumping in and going head over heals in, or build rings of hay for 'houses' and rest, unwittingly having given help to the welfare of the Park horses. We would return home, hot and sticky, prickled all over by grass stalks and covered in seed, but how is it none of us suffered from hay-fever as a result of these activities.

I was not very old when I became distinctly aware of the Park Keeper. He was Mr. Bates, a man to be respected and very smart in his blue uniform with silver adornments. Through a friend's father, I got to know him a little and found him to be a gentle man, proud of his park about which he was an expert, and a keen naturalist. Now the assistant park-keeper was a different kettle of fish. I don't know his name except that we called him 'Ginger'. He may have been as pleasant as his chief but to small boys he was someone to be feared and avoided. At approaching twilight, the duty keeper would walk round the Park blowing his whistle to indicate that the Park was about to be cleared and the gates locked. As soon as we heard the sound, we would stop our game and proceed smartly to the nearest gate, but at the double when Ginger was on duty. Later, but not in the twenties I experienced the excitement of crossing the Park in the dark, risking dire trouble. Ginger boxed my ears once; I had not noticed him as I walked alone across the Park in my Sunday best and I took a small ball from my pocket and kicked it a couple of times. As Ginger clouted me, he asked sternly, 'Don't you know that you don't play with a ball on Sunday?' I never committed the outrage again.

At an early age I knew every corner of the Park. The woods behind the Mansion were strongly fenced, but there was a small fringe near Water Road, which was outside of the fence and here I have shot a thousand Germans and captured as many Red Indians. Unfortunately, this area was on a slope and I had frequent falls and my clothes were muddied which would mean trouble later. Mr. Bates did give permission for grown-ups to take their children blue-belling in the woods, but this was restricted to the influential few. Around the pond was a splendid place for stalking and hiding and seeking, but disaster came near to me, there. My next door neighbour's nephew was staying with his Aunt and he and I took out her dog, Barney, who decided to take the opportunity provided by the ice covered water, to explore the little island. On his return journey, Barney fell through the ice and could not get out. We tried to reach him on the ice but nearly joined him. We went to the Mansion and a man came down with a ladder and yanked Barney out. I am afraid the man was an unrewarded hero. The dog could not stand; we wrapped him in our overcoats and carried him home. He fully recovered.

What infinite activities were to be enjoyed in the Park! We snowballed there, we tobogganed on make-shift arrangements down the slope below the Mansion. We climbed trees; we played marbles; we threw sticks up at the horse-chestnut trees and subsequently played conkers. We caught frogs; we disturbed a wild bees nest (only once, as this proved to be a painful activity) and we rattled sticks along the wooden fences of houses in Liebenrood Rd. We caught newts in the out of bounds area in the S.E. corner; we crossed the private strip of farmland, crawling on our stomachs to the copse bordering Honey End Lane. We picked mushrooms; we played in Dick Turpin's hideout, which went under the Bath Road (the A4 to you), a tunnel which some foolish adults thought was a drain for the lower part of the Park. Many of these sports were interrupted by the strident voice of authority as was my favourite pastime football, if we played between the football posts on the most important pitches.

Prospect Park between the wars. At that time the grass was left uncut between the end of the football season and haymaking in June, giving it a more naturally rural appearance. (Courtesy of Reading Museum & Art Gallery).

Somehow we always managed to have a football. I had one, a worn out one from a local club, but what a tragedy it was, when big boys punched it from under my arm as I was crawling home. I never saw it again but I can still feel the pain. We had rules for any number of players; eight was a good number with 4 pairs - score 3 goals and your pair went in goal. I must have run miles and miles, playing like a demon, to get the ball between 2 piles of coats. (Oh! The arguments about whether it was inside, outside or rebounded from the 'post'). Most winter afternoons the Reading F.C. players walked across the park and how we showed off when any of them looked our way and what pride when one of them kicked our ball back to us. There were no football shorts worn; we just wore out old trousers - short ones but rather on the long side. Not surprisingly, our legs, on the inside in particular became chapped and it needed a bandy-legged style of walking to reach home. Washing off the mud was painful and Snowfire or Melrose rubbed on made it worse before it got better. I wonder how many hours I played football in this way before I played for a team.

Summer time was the time for picnicking. We children used to play in the Park and then, later in the afternoon, our mothers joined us for a picnic. It must have been when I was 6 that I had by birthday party in the Park; sandwiches, cakes and real lemonade and jolly games. I can remember getting over-excited and being a nuisance, especially about the fairness in the games. My mother let the others win and I couldn't stand for that! The other summer bonus was the Stop Me & Buy One ice-cream tricycles waiting at the Park entrance and a penny Snowfruit, often bought with coins that I looked for regularly and sometimes found around the Park seats .

There was just one part of the Park I avoided. The part close to 'The Fever Hospital', near Cockney Hill, filled me with horror. I had grown up, listening to harrowing tales of children with 'the fever', (I had no idea what this was) being taken inside where they would remain indefinitely, away from all outside contacts. The thought of this lack of freedom appalled me and the hospital became for me a place of doom with certainty when I witnessed a dog being run over and killed outside the gates. Fortunately, my mind concentrated on the joys of Prospect Park and not on this unhappy corner.

When I think of my childhood, I think of the Park. With all the advantages children have today, I do not envy them one little bit.

Many of my contemporaries have also expressed appreciation of Reading's Parks and the joy the parks added to their childhood. Some of their memories were new to me and the detail often amazed me. Mrs. C.M. Page of Wantage Road remembers seeing Mr. Bates, the park-keeper of Prospect Park, searching for and selecting turves of grass from around the park to provide the fine grass for his beautiful bowling green. She also recalls the line of railings and hawthorn bushes from the Mansion to the Bath Road which provided two separate areas of grazing for sheep. I have been reminded of the pleasure we gained from our home-made bats and balls and from our bottle of cold tea and our bottle of water for the lemonade powder.

I remember several agricultural shows in Prospect Park and I enjoyed the recollection of May Tapp of Holberton Road, who 60 years ago benefited from the cows on show in the Park whose owners were glad to distribute free milk to anyone with an empty beer bottle. Several glorious days of rice pudding followed this activity.

Mr. D.E. Davis of Sudbury witnessed a parachute jump at the August fete in Prospect Park during the 1920s. Unfortunately the parachutist landed in a tree near the Cunning Man in Burghfield Road.

A visit to the Park revives my happy memories of long ago and therefore I have the feeling that Prospect Park is just the same as ever. Mr. W.F. Champion of Drayton Road disagreed with me. He says that all has changed except the size - 88 acres. Many elms ahve gone, the mansion is sadly faded, there are no longer any flower beds and the view towards the Kennet Valley from the hill is ruined by housing and towering blocks of flats. Mr. Champion is prepared to fight for the preservation of Prospect Park. All of us can be relieved to know that we have Prospect Park's Champion at the ready.

Interesting Characters

As a child and being one of many fatherless boys after the 1914-18 War, I was shy in the company of men. Even so, several local artisans, respectable, reliable, typical of the terraced house dwellers of Reading in the twenties, had an important influence on me. There was a retired coach man, small and articulate, who used to pontificate in my presence about the importance of one's appearance. I was much impressed by his neat white beard, his natty suits, gleaming boots and brown bowler, set at a jaunty angle. Cleanliness was the lesson from a war veteran, a machine gunner who had suffered long deprivation in the trenches and afterwards valued highly, perhaps not entirely rationally, the value of soap and water, clean finger nails and clean hair. Again, he played his part in influencing a small Reading boy. My impression of fathers was that they were kindly, generous men who gave stability to their families. I may have been looking at the situation through rose coloured spectacles but I believe that generally speaking this is how things were, a reaction to the horrors of the war.

In particular, there was the steady, reliable train driver who went off in his pale blue dungarees, peaked cap and tin box to man his engine somewhere in the vast area of steaming engines, sidings, shunting goods wagons and coal trucks, operating noisily both day and night in a complex of railway lines west of Reading Station. I admired him not only because he had driven the 'Caerphilly Castle', and he played a small part in my development. Similarly, I thought well of the local window cleaner. He cycled around the West End of Reading, bucket and chamois on the handlebars and with ladder perched on his shoulder. Apart from this admirable performance and occupation, he was the local lamp-lighter. Again he cycled around and as far as I could tell, seven evenings a week, he would raise his pole whilst mounted on his steed like Don Quixote, strike the lamp just at the right spot and ignite the gas in the street lamps. In fog, rain, wind and snow, he was there. What a model of dependability he was. My headmistress terrified me and I am sure that I never uttered more than a monosyllable to her. But she was fair and I respected her. She rescued me on one occasion from a confrontation with boys from a neighbouring school who were about to make life unpleasant for me. She scared them too. They didn't bother me again. Then there was my grandfather; he looked like a retired colonel but was not anything so grand. I was concious that he liked children, enjoyed their mischief and shared their joy. He certainly never struck me and I cannot remember him admonishing me; he was very honest, well groomed, proud of his family and hard working. I suppose I have some part of me which is him.

Then there were the lesser lights who made their mark upon me. One of the insults boys threw at each other in the twenties was, 'You're going to be a dung boy!' Dung boys in Reading wore simple red uniform and a pill box hat. They pushed stout red carts and armed with a broom and shovel cleared up the main Reading streets after the horse traffic had passed. These lads looked all right to me but early prejudice had been sown. I was sure I was not going to become a dung-boy. In the twenties any road work was guarded at night by a watchman who sat in a small sentry box like hut, facing a coke fire in a brazier. His main job was to keep alight the oil lamps which surrounded the upheaval. I noted that we relied upon these men to get safely from A to B.

'Gipsy Smith' at the door of her caravan in George Street, later the site of G.R. Jackson's 'Bottle & Jar' store.

Battle Hospital and around was the Workhouse. The unsmiling, well scrubbed, basically dressed inmates of all ages were a frightening sight to those of us whose destiny was not very clear, but the destitutes who gathered outside each night were the material of nightmares. Many who gathered in Oxford Road were victims of the war: the crippled, the shell-shocked and the deranged, and others who were simple minded. I would scuttle past them, trying not to notice the poverty, the sickness and hopelessness. One or two seemed attracted to Reading and were always around. The noisy, ranting Jock with the ribbons of his glengarry flying was someone I avoided; he embarrassed me. Then there was Sam. His presence must have done something to me. I can see him clearly, although I saw him for the last time well over half a century ago. This tall gaunt figure wandered in the Prospect Park area, dressed in his tattered army coat, unkempt and with his few belongings including an empty cocoa tin on a piece of string. The call from boys was 'Sam, Sam, the dirty old man, washed his face in a frying pan!' But he used to smile, sadly but pleasantly as we passed him. I am certain he was kindly. I wish I had had the courage to speak to him. He was found dead in an allotment hut.

With the help of 'Midweek' readers, what a crowd of odd characters in Reading in the twenties have come to mind.

All of these have been remembered. - The rag and bone man who used to push his truck walking on his tip toes and blowing his bugle at the corner of each street.

Tommy, a little man who sported a splendid red coat when he followed the local hunts with great enthusiasm.

The old man who ran down the pitch at Elm Park during the half time interval, merely for the purpose of giving us the opportunity to throw rubbish at him.

The coloured gentleman who had a pitch in the Market Place on Saturdays and, to encourage the sale of his toothpaste, offered to take out teeth, free of charge. There were takers of this generous offer in spite of the crowd which would gather to

34

watch the operations.

The pretty Italian ice cream girls selling ice cream not surpassed today.

The hurdy-gurdy man, thought to have been called Petulango with his little monkey dressed in a little red coat and a round hat.

How did two women become to be named Footsack and Toerag? They were usually involved in collecting rags, bones and rabbit skins and carrying their gains away in sacks, but Footsack was seen selling home-made iron holders in Broad Street at one penny each.

Mrs. Seeley recalled the flower lady of 60 years ago who sold her wares from door to door and was known as Liza-sez-she. The name was given to her because of her enjoying a good chat and telling what her 'ladies' (customers) had said to her and so beginning her tales with, 'Liza-sez-she'. . . . Mr. Joseph Francis was able to give more information about her. Although known as Liza, her real name was Lottie Ming whose father was a gardener at Waterer's Nursery at the Floral Mile. She was the mother of Charlie Ming who kept an egg n' poultry shop, Dickensian in character, in Southampton Street.

Two or three times a year the two 'Fern Ladies' called at doors in Reading; they offered ferns for a bundle of old clothes and were considered to give good value for worn out cast-offs.

Also seen in many parts of Reading during the twenties was the Cats' Meat Man, touring the streets with his long pointed stick spiking slices of horse meat.

Considered to be at least unusual was the man who used to keep cows in Wilson Road and grew mangolds nearby to feed his stock and sold the milk locally.

Harry Currants was harmless, good with young children but reacted angrily to older children calling after him. He was supposed to have gained this name when he was caught stealing currants from a shop.

The moral of this story must be that if you want to be remembered in 60 years time, be a little odd or unusual and some one may write about you many years hence. But really I should say thank you to all these Reading folk of the past for the experience of meeting you and helping me to understand human frailty.

Walking along the quieter stretches of the river, you might be rewarded by the occasional sighting of jumping fish, herons or even a kingfisher.

The Thames

If asked at school 'For what is Reading famous?', the answer would be Suttons' seeds, Huntley & Palmers' biscuits, Simmonds' beer and the river Thames. When young, there was no doubt in my mind that these products were the best in the world and that the greatest river was the Thames. This meant the stretch of water between Tilehurst Station and Sonning Lock. As far as I was concerned Old Father Thames, whose company was to be enjoyed seriously, lived in Reading. In my early days I was walked, as were many more young people, on a Sunday in particular, from Caversham Bridge to Scours Lane or from there to the Roebuck and back again. It was all very sober and proper and our Sunday best clothes allowed little scope for behaviour other than what was expected of a small boy on the Sabbath. Even so, I enjoyed sights and sounds on and under the banks of the Thames at Reading. As a Bank Holiday treat, we would walk from Reading Lock to Sonning Lock and return on the bus. My memory of these occasions is clearly of crowds of families enjoying the same activity. The special treat was a trip on a steamer. On half a dozen Sundays in my early years, I sat and hardly moved on the *Starlight* as I absorbed the excitement of a return trip from the Bridge to Tilehurst Station. It was sixpence for kids - 2½p! Just once or twice, I went further afloat on a larger steamer, the *Majestic* and was given the lasting pleasure of seeing Thames-side lawns sweeping down to the water-side. But there was a worrying feature of these river trips. Each boat was accompanied by a few ragged boys who ran along the towpath for the duration of the trip. They performed cartwheels, hand-stands, head-stands and forward rolls and did daring deeds on the top of the occasional gate and finally dived in the water as the boat 'docked' to gather the few pennies thrown to them. I was disturbed by these children and preferred to look the other way. I was saddened by the thought that all that effort might produce little reward.

Boating on the Thames was a leisurely recreation; men were dressed predominantly in 'whites' and their ladies lounged elegantly amongst the cushions, displaying their flowered frocks and picturesque hats and protecting their complexions under parasols. The younger element showed their strength in skiffs and many Reading lads were efficient with a pair of oars.

Punts were most common and were often 'poled' along, although my admiration was for the lone punt boatman with the single paddle. This skill I came to appreciate even more when I tried to propel my punt and girl-friend single handed, years later. Motor-boats were few and of the type seen carrying the umpire at Henley Regatta, sleek and aristocratic, built for short relaxing voyages of a mile or two. Motor-boats were accepted with meagre grace by the self propelled boating fraternity and they were greeted with calls, 'Please mind your wash, sir'; a request which received polite response then but which fails to be understood now. When I was in a punt recently, it was quickly filled with water from the wash of speedy motor boats and I sat in water most of the time. Steamer captains were more careful of lesser craft but smuts from the funnels were an annoyance.

When old enough to explore the Thames river banks unaccompanied, I fished with a net and a jam-jar. Minnows could be caught but it needed patience and subtlety. There was a rewarding spot at an outflow pipe from the ice factory between the two bridges. However, I was quite content to sit on the bank in a quiet and lonely spot watching the swans, moorhens, coots, swooping swallows and martins, dragon and damsel flies. Occasionally I saw a heron, a jumping fish, a vole and sometimes a kingfisher, especially when trespassing on to the north bank via the Warren. In the twenties, music from a gramophone was far from being high fidelity, but

The iron bridge of 1869 at Caversham. The new bridge opened in 1926 without the planned ceremony by the Prince of Wales, owing to the impact of the General Strike.

across the river waters the imperfections were mainly dispelled and these sounds on a still summer's evening from a craft holding the elite, filled me with an ambition. And even more so, the sight of the camping punt with its iron frame and furled green canvas for night protection. In later years, I was not disappointed by experience.

There were flood times when most of the Promenade was under water and so was Grant's or Battle Farm when they stretched as far as Audley Street and Salisbury Road and the cows came under the two railway bridges in Cow Lane to be milked only a short distance from Oxford Road. At this time there was no through road to the river. Sometimes the Reading Temperance Band played on the Prom and crowds which gathered to listen were considerable. There were recognised bathing places - or at least places recognised by my generation. Bathing costumes were not a necessity but the lack of them required some subterfuge in entering the water and making a quick exit.

At the age of ten, I could recite the names of all of the principal rivers in England - Tyne, Wear, Tees, Ouse, Trent . . . . . . What a waste of time, I used to think, when I know where the best river in the world is. It's the Thames at Reading!

In the twenties, boating was a leisurely restful pursuit, quite different from the modern queues at locks separated by mad rushes to get to the next one first. Whereas today's music beating out from cruisers does not suit the occasion, records from a wind-up gramophone of the twenties, filtering across a summer evening's air, contributed to the serenity of the scene. Jack Buchanan quietly romanticising from beneath the weeping willows for instance.

It won't be the same again; but just as well, as the former Chief Constable of Reading, Mr. Jesse Lawrence wrote, reminding us that in February 1929, the Thames at Reading froze right the way across and skating on the ice was enjoyed by large crowds for several days. Mr. Lawrence remembers it well as he was doing a month's night duty early in his career and he wondered if he had been very clever in joining the police as he took his midnight refreshment, as was customary then, in the shelter of a shop doorway.

A trip on a river steamer in about 1924. One of the small girls in the photograph remembers after 60 years this occasion as one of the most exciting days of her childhood. Although a hot summer day, everyone is formally dressed complete with hats.

Caversham Lock was often the starting point for a Bank Holiday trip. Some families enjoyed a sedate walk in 'Sunday Best' from here to Sonning Lock, returning by bus if funds allowed.

How much better the waters of the Thames must be controlled at the present time. Most inhabitants of Reading would now be unaware of the small areas of the river that were often flooded but so many of you from Caversham, the Caversham Road area, the Great Knollys Street area and parts of West Reading were seriously affected during your childhood. I have been reminded of Joey Keel who let out punts and row boats at the end of Scours Lane. He lived above his boat house and in winter he would often row up Scours Lane to Oxford Road to purchase stores.

I suppose that my term for the young boys who ran along the tow-path keeping up with the steamers was too strong. There has been some objection to my calling them 'ragged urchins'. It is quite a relief to know these boys survived and made good; they apparently enjoyed their 3 and 4 miles run and the coppers that they were awarded at the end of the trip.

Mention has been made of Dr. Fosbury's Sunday School in Valentia Road and the Sunday School outings which were frequently on the river steamer to Streatley. It was a very special day for many children in the 1920s. I remember Dr. Fosbury well; he had a surgery nearly opposite Elm Park Hall in Oxford Road and he was an imposing gentleman, Victorian in dress and bearded. I was his patient when very small, about 3, and over-awed by him, but his removal of my vest, saying 'skin a rabbit!' put me entirely at ease. They call such an action now child psychology, but to Dr. Fosbury it just came naturally.

We all had our favourite river steamers. According to the names of the boats which have been remembered, there were a lot of them and several firms owned them. Salter Bros. had the Oxford to Kingston boats and then there were Maynard's boats and Cawston's boats. Sunday afternoon near Caversham Bridge, Charlie Maynard could be heard directing customers to the *Britannia* with 'The White boat for Goring' and Mr. Cawston would parry with 'The Brown Boat for Henley' and point towards the *Majestic*. Memories of *The Queen of the Thames* also survive; she was built locally but was damaged when launched and had to be repaired before she worked. She is now recorded sadly as Conservancy Wreck No. 12 near Windsor.

Mr. F.C. Rimes of Horndean Road, whose

father was in charge of East's Boathouse at the Bridge, later taken over by Cawston's and now the headquarters of Reading Rowing Club, recalls very busy Sundays. A fine afternoon would encourage hundreds of Reading folk on to the river - 10/- all day! He and his father would prepare all the boats before breakfast. Monday morning was spent looking for missing boats still moored up river to avoid payment. And they solved the trouble in the same way as supermarkets today deal with trolley loss; they introduced a £1 deposit.

I have been told that steamers were not unknown to run out of coals and to limp home, using the wooden furniture as fuel. Other information given includes - Reading F.C. Players and staff frequently had an outing on a steamer. Two motor-boats of the twenties, the *Magician* and *Enchantress* are still in use as umpire boats at regattas.

It has been thought that I should have made more reference to the Kennet and its importance to Reading. I knew the Kennet and the Canal from Reading to Aldermaston even better than I knew the Thames. For hundreds of hours I have wandered in this area and to assure all of my readers of my regard for the Kennet-Avon Canal I record that my wife and I, when both over 65, walked from Newbury to Bristol, 77 miles in 6 days! As a result I can assure Mr. George Gray of Foxhays Road that restoration work is going on all along the canal. He says that he welcomes efforts to restore the upper reaches and is looking forward to travelling by water from Reading to Devizes. Mr. Gray's father and grandfather owned narrow boats on the Kennet and he remembers busy scenes in Reading where these boats were loaded and unloaded.

I was beginning to think I was the only one who called the area the other side of the railway to Southcote, the Wire-mills. I never knew why I called it that. I was so pleased to hear from Mrs. W. Smith of Mortimer, saying that her address was the Wire-mills. Her husband was the lock-keeper and responsible for the river and canal from Theale to Fobney Pumping Station. I knew this wonderful piece of countryside before she did and can understand that she does not wish to return now that her cottage has gone, but I must go there again and re-create it in my mind.

A Wilson Central School Outing 1920/22. This was a very special day for many schoolchildren between the wars.

The river at Pangbourne. This is the spot which some luckier children in the twenties and thirties visited on Bank Holidays. The splendid houses looking across the river were built without any thought that within a few decades the lonely lane in front of them would become a main road, with all its attendant noise and nuisance.

The Aftermath of the Great War

Being born during the Great War gave one an impression of remembering it. Of course I do not remember it, but a synthesis of what I saw, when young, in the streets of Reading and what I overheard of hushed and despairing conversations, gave me a feeling later of experiencing the war. Those early years certainly had an influence on my life and on my thinking. The dreaded telegraph boy had brought the news of my father's death in France and my mother would speak bitterly of the Front, life in the trenches and the Germans. With the help of what I saw of the aftermath of war in Reading, my imagination reached the horrors of 'going over the top'. I watched the Red Cross ambulances streaming constantly along the Oxford Road, to and from hospitals and converted schools such as Battle School. I was familiar, too, with groups of servicemen in hospital blue, minimising their injuries and missing limbs; meeting them in the streets of Reading was overwhelming for a small boy because they greeted everyone with enforced exuberance. Most disturbing was the regular meeting in the Bath Road or in Tilehurst Road of a pretty young wife leading her tall, blinded husband with the mutilated face. And then there was the unmoving body in the long wickerwork wheeled chair. I did not want to look at this kind of sight that I saw all too frequently in the streets of Reading, but I did and the impact of seeing the tragic aftermath of the war and the feelings it stirred are still with me. My memories of the early twenties and Reading are all in the colour of grey. I am sure it was not so, but I recall Broad Street and elsewhere without colour. Obviously, there were many still in mourning, but Reading was to me at seven years old, a town of grey caps, grey window-blinds, grey dogs, grey aprons, grey fashions, all and everyone grey - a fantasy perhaps, but that was the mood of Reading after the war. The 'musicians' in Broad Street (and there were many of them) frequently more than one group at a time, played their merry tunes but the joy they brought to a small boy was tempered by their lack of limbs and rows of medals as they collected a few pennies for survival. Most alarming to me was the 'the ex' soldier with no pension, escaping by convulsive jerks from a straight jacket, earning very little in spite of his excessive efforts on a gravelly path near Reading Bridge.

In my early years, I was conscious that there were not many men about in Reading. I was friendly with Arthur, Buddy, Doug, Noel, Sam, Joe, Trevor and Fred; we hadn't a dad between us and so my contact with men was limited. As a result, I was uncomfortable and tongue-tied in their presence. I was anxious to please them, to avoid them and to escape from their attention. Male school teachers were an anathema; the huge Reading policemen of the twenties filled me with awe; commissionaires, bus conductors, shop walkers, park-keepers, swimming-bath attendants, doctors, ticket-collectors, car-owners. In fact, most men were in authority and small boys in Reading then did not wait to be told twice to do anything by anyone in authority.

The war was over but things were not right. I knew — Reading was not yet a happy place again, but I did not understand. There must have been widows in every side street of Oxford Road, King's Road, London Road and Wokingham Road and each would tell their orphan children that their fathers had died to make the world a better place. Quite early I found this premise incompatible with the poverty I saw in Silver

A group of Australian war-wounded soldiers at Wilson School which was used after World War I as one of the convalescent homes for troops. On the right is Mr H.E. White who as a young lad used to run errands for the injured soldiers.

Street, Great Knollys Street, Brunswick Street and elsewhere. I thought it strange that there were doctors but that there were times when we could not afford them. Most disturbing were the Welsh coal-miners, marching through Reading on their way to London; gaunt men, hollow cheeked with heavily lined faces, ill fed, poorly clad, only a muffler extra in winter to their summer clothes, and their eyes showing little joy of life. I saw copies of *The Illustrated War News,* showing the British spirit during the Great War. But at the age of seven or eight, I had seen enough in Reading to understand that there was nothing great about war.

Politics was something that did not impinge on the lives of us children, but I remember some of the rhymes which we chanted at election times. I wonder who originated the political rhymes for the children of the twenties to chant. We all called out these rhymes so lustily that one suspects that the political parties invented them to gain some free publicity.

Basically they followed this pattern.

> Vote, vote for Leslie Wilson,
> Chuck old Asquith in the sea,
> If we had a lump of lead,
> We would chuck it at his head,
> And he would not come voting any more.

For Leslie Wilson, we substituted Dr. Hastings and Mr. Keyser (the squire of Aldermaston Court) and alternatives for line 3 and 4 were -

> 'If it wasn't for the law
> We'd sock him in the jaw.'

Children in several parts of Reading received part-time schooling, even when the war was over, because their schools were being used as hospitals and convalescent homes for British soldiers and for soldiers from countries within the British Empire. Hospital blue was to be seen around Battle School and Wilson School, and Harry White of Tilehurst has recorded his association with Australian soldiers at Wilson School. He used to run errands, often fetching fish and chips for them from Mr. & Mrs Beckford's shop in Wilson Road, where he was rewarded with a bag of 'crinklings', pieces of crispy batter which had become detached from the frying fish. Mr. White as a small boy had his good service rewarded by being invited to have his photograph taken with these soldiers.

West Reading Library at the end of the war was a resting place for invalid soldiers, and groups of children used to gather around them for a chat and some children took on the task of cleaning the soldiers' boots. Children also used to gather in Cow Lane when troop trains were being organised before the journey to the continent. The youngsters would wave and cheer but the main attraction for them was the odd biscuit or sweet thrown from the train window and for which they would scramble. There was evidence that the children brought solace before and after battle.

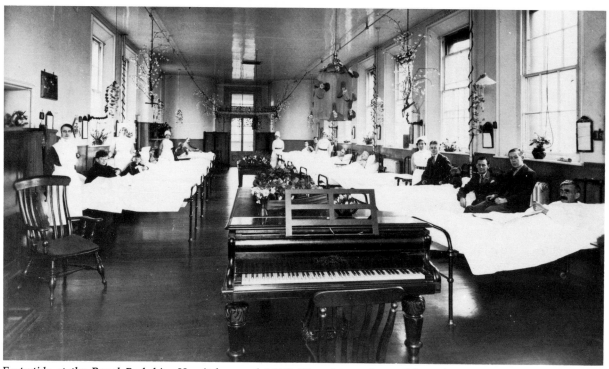

Eastertide at the Royal Berkshire Hospital around 1930. The picture shows Sidmouth ward complete with seasonal decorations made by the patients themselves.

They Delivered to the Door!

We are fortunate in this country to have milk daily to our homes. In the twenties, this service was accepted without proper appreciation, just as it is now, but then we had two deliveries: the first one before Reading awoke and the second later in the day, to make sure we had enough for the remainder of meals. At night, the lidded pewter can was put outside the front door and in the early hours the milkman filled it with his ladle with milk from his large can, which was refilled from time to time from a churn. Several milkmen delivered in our street - Williams, Onyett's and the Co-op. I remember them, all with their shiny carts or 'prams', loaded with an assortment of cans and measures around the polished brass churn.

Bread, too, was delivered daily and there were several bakers from which to choose. Our baker's cart was large and smart. He hooked loaves from the far end of his cart, filled his basket and presented his customers with an interesting choice of cottage loaf, coburg, milk, tin, brown, currant, etc. His horse was always given its bag of oats outside our house and as it shook it about to reach the tastiest morsels it spilled some and a few enterprising sparrows were always nearby to take advantage of this habit. The horse often left its mark in the road and it was my task to collect it with bucket and shovel for the benefit of our small garden.

I think I am right in saying that the Coal Union man called fortnightly. He was paid a shilling a week all the year round, and this paid for a ton of coal and more. A few logs were delivered as well; both coal and logs being carried by the simplest form of four-wheeled cart. The rubbish was taken away in a stout high sided two-wheeled cart drawn by a heavy horse with jangling basses. We also had a mobile green-grocer — a very obliging man who would return to his rickety cart to weigh up the smallest quantity of fruit or greens. We used to add a little stale bread to his horse's diet of the outer leaves of cabbages and unsaleable oddments because he looked to be in need of extra nourishment. There was the rag 'n bone man. He pushed his cart regularly down our way and a bag of worn out clothes, a few jam jars, a rabbit skin or a pile of newspapers would bring us a few extra coppers. There was the butcher-cum-fishmonger, but my mother remained loyal to Mr. Brewer, the butcher at the corner of our road. Delivery vans came and went; even in our street small orders were delivered. The Co-op and Baylis' delivered little boxes of groceries, Colebrooks' delivered the weekly leg of lamb, McIlroys & Bulls delivered the altered coat and errand boys were used by the smaller businesses. Sunday was the day for the muffin man, carrying his tray of wares on his head and ringing his hand bell to tell us that it was time to get our crumpets for tea.

The street was a busy scene, with every trade duplicated and and where the service of free delivery was given to customers without question. Consequently, the noise of hooves on the tarmac was considerable and this led to a custom which I regarded as the height of respectability; the covering of the road with used bark from the tanneries outside a house where someone who was ill needed quiet.

It was not unknown for the corner shops to deliver even quite small purchases, all part of good service. It should be stressed that the corner shop played an important part in a housewife's life in the twenties. It's only slightly an exaggeration to say that in the side streets of Reading, every corner had a shop and there were

Mr 'Mick' McColm, driving one of Venner's lorries in the 1930s. This particular photograph was used to advertise Michelin tyres before the Second World War.

others in between as well. Today, young housewives pay at the supermarket check-out by cheque and frequently for an amount equal to about half of a 1920 husband's annual income. The corner shop provided a day to day supply of essentials as a few coppers accrued, or were allowed to be obtained on the 'slate'. They were often extraordinary shops, stocked to the ceiling and giving forth a multitude of varied smells. Mrs. Sopp, a wonderfully warm character, in her shop in Brunswick Street could sell you any small item under the sun and patiently serve you with toffees for 1d., a pickled onion, a handful of biscuits or a slice of bread pudding and supply you with an up-turned mineral-water crate to sit on, while you ate your snack. Are there any shops today which across one counter, could supply you with a gob stopper, a yard of elastic, 5 Woodbines, a pair of shirt studs and a teat for a baby's bottle?

Most deliveries made were done efficiently but at a comfortable speed. I remember that Downings delivered firewood, soda, matches and paraffin in particular, as well as other hardware items at break-neck speed from their van. Their service was excellent from the smelly old van.

On a summer's day, when all the bustle of these delivery carts and vans was over, along our road would come the water cart, a giant horse drawn watering-can, laying the dust at the end of the day. Here was another chance of fun for we young ones; we darted in and out of the spray, cooling ourselves at the expense of our clothes.

Reading Trams

They were noisy, grinding and grunting, while jogging and jostling their passengers who sat on hard uncomfortable seats; but every moment of a penny ride on a Reading tram was bliss indeed to me as a boy. Even greater was the pleasure, when having walked 'up town', my mother could afford the twopenny fares for our homeward journey, so avoiding the over-familiar walk. Sometimes, we had to save a penny and so only 'tram' from Russell Street to Elm Park Road. We usually rode inside (and I was always made to give up my seat to a lady) but occasionally we climbed the steep, open twisting stairs to the uncovered top of the tram, where we staggered to our seat with the adjustable back, changing it from one side to another so that we could face the way we were going. Best of all was the conductor's shout on a wet day 'On top only'. Then we wiped our damp seat with a handkerchief and sat with the rain beating in our faces. What a nuisance it was when my mother put up her umbrella; she did not appreciate the exhilaration of being open to the elements. There was the thrill, too, of passing under the Oxford Road railway bridge. 'Keep your seats', it said on the board above and I often wondered if one's head would be knocked off if one stood up. The obvious dip in the road, which always flooded in winter, suggested a close fit, but no one ever stood up to satisfy a small boy's curiosity.

The trams never turned around at the termini; only the driver changed from one end to the other while the conductor turned around the arm, high in the air, to the overhead electricity supply. Even at a tender age, I noticed the lack of ingenuity by the designers in planning that this task should have to be done with the aid of an unmanageable pole and many false shots. I thought about inventing a better system but I realised that an improved electricity supply might put an end to the sizzling and flying sparks and I didn't want that.

I knew nearly all of the tram-drivers by sight, I admired their fortitude and sometimes I felt sad that their lot was not a better one. No windscreen for them; they stood there all day, protected to the waist only, facing all weathers, grasping the two control handles with hands encased in enormous gloves. I suppose that I never wished to be a tram driver because I had seen their faces snow covered, and their moustaches dripping little icicles. But I would have liked to have 'had a go'. It looked so easy, with no steering to worry about, only the two brass handles, one to go and one to stop and turn around with a great flourish. And the two pedals; one to ring the warning bell and rung with urgency for the hapless cyclist caught in the tram-lines. The other was a mystery to me in my early years, until I alighted at a terminus one day and managed to step on the pedal unnoticed. All was revealed when the tram drew away. A little pile of gritty sand appeared in the tram-line. The sand enabled the tram to get a grip when the lines were iced.

However could I have imagined that their routes were long? But I did. From the Pond House to the Three Tuns had the same feeling for me as Gatwick to Minorca does now. It was, then, from the countryside to countryside. One tram would go along the Wokingham Road and the next, after a quick alteration to the points by the driver with a simple lever, would go along the London Road for a distance hardly worth the bother, to the railway bridge. The journey from Caversham Bridge to Whitley Pump was shorter but there was always the doubt about the tram ever reaching the top of

Once a familiar sight in the town, tramcars are now just a nostalgic memory. This picture was taken in St. Mary's Butts around 1920.

West Reading railway bridge over Oxford Road, looking towards the town. The sign 'Keep Your Seats' is a warning to passengers riding on the top of the tramcars. One can be seen just to the right of centre

Southampton Street. How cold it was 'on top' facing the north wind going down hill in winter. One more route went from the town to Erleigh Road but I was convinced that this route was not for the likes of me. It did not serve the kind of streets I knew. Surely, one could only board this tram if one travelled 1st class on the G.W.R. I equated these trams with the 'Caerphilly Castle' - the supertrain of the twenties.

The Mill Lane Depot and its surrounds were more fascinating at busy times than any 'Spaghetti Junction' and to be watched patiently for collisions that never happened. Best of all was the advance of hordes of trams, bearing boards on the fronts of them announcing, 'Football Special'. On Saturday afternoons they were nose to tail from Broad Street to Kensington Road where they disgorged a sober and drab crowd of cloth-capped Reading supporters.

Strangely enough, I can never remember waiting for a tram; they must have been very frequent. Is it a pity we have no trams now? What chaos they would cause - middle of the road drivers - and would we ever get safely from pavement to the steps of the tram? Still, I would like to buy a bag of hot chestnuts or a hot potato in the Butts and eat them on top of the tram just once more for old times' sake, and receive one of the coloured tickets drawn from the conductors clipboard and punched to the sound of a bell.

Most of the letters I have received concerning the trams of Reading refer to drivers and conductors as 'great characters' and emphasise that they were important ingredients of the pleasure of riding on a tram. At the termini, regular passengers, scurrying around a corner and in danger of being late for work, were waited for by a sympathetic tram crew and there would be much banter as the breathless passenger climbed the steps. Leslie Harris had a particular delight - the 'bogie' cars, numbers 31 to 36 and he enjoyed the fun of standing upstairs or downstairs to accommodate everyone. G.A. Ayres of Blewbury records two delightful 'inside stories' about tramwaymen. As they worked long hours, their supper, including a blue enamel can

A tram on the route to Whitley. Many a hapless cyclist would get his wheels caught in the tram lines, whereupon the conductor would sound the warning bell with real urgency.

of tea, was sent to them and deposited in a green wooden box permanently in position outside the Street. Often children would deliver their dad's supper to other tram drivers who would put it in the green box so that dad could collect his supper as he reached the West Street/Broad Street junction. The second story is of a secret revealed! The conductor showed great ingenuity by inventing the system of wearing, upside down around the tops of his thighs, a pair of men's suspenders which he fastened to the bottom of his very thick vest. This prevented the discomfort caused by the vest riding up his body as the result of having to pull down and reverse the conductor pole at the end of every trip.

Happy days! But we have all forgotten how bitter cold it was on a Reading tram on a cold winter's night.

A tram conductress during the 1914–1918 War. The long heavy skirt must have been a nuisance when going upstairs to collect fares.

Reading F.C. during the 1920-21 season, when the Royals were the founder members of the original Division Three. A year later they went on to join Division Three South for five years before they eventually gained promotion to Division Two.

A Reading F.C. Supporter

My mother and grandma used to sit in the front room to watch the football crowds going up our road on a Saturday afternoon. My grandfather was a great Reading supporter and in my very young days I thought all men of Reading went to Elm Park on Saturdays. My first appreciation of 'football days' came as a result of the little shop next door and the stall the shop-keeper put outside the facilitate the quick sale of sweets and cigarettes. I would stand on the far side of the stall waiting for the sale of a packet of cigarettes so that I could approach the buyer with my 'Cigarette card please mister'. This activity helped me to have many complete sets. Later in the afternoon, I moved to Norfolk Road to be ready for the gates being opened ten minutes before the end of the game; we youngsters all rushed in to see the final stage of matches. Eventually I went to matches with my grandfather, he with his trilby and walking-stick, standing a few paces behind me standing close to the iron railings surrounding the pitch. The crowd, mostly cloth capped, were vociferous but orderly and well-behaved, and the banter between rival supporters was humorous and harmless. For most of those at Elm Park in the twenties, this was the brief release from rather a hard life.

I think the ground must have opened earlier

in those days. I know I was in the ground hours before Kick-off of the big matches. The year Reading were beaten by Cardiff 3-0 in the semi-final of the Cup, I saw the first of three encounters with Manchester Utd. and I remember taking my dinner and tea with me. I was going with my friends by this time, my grandfather sitting in the stand. I think he might have still been on the terraces but he won a £3 stand ticket in a competition in the 'Football Echo', a forerunner of the 'pools'. He forecast all of '12 results' correctly!!

Most of the players were in 'digs' in West Reading and I saw a lot of them off the field. I regarded Duckworth as the greatest goal-keeper, Eggo as the steadiest of defenders, McConnell as the player who might have been one of the great players if he had not had his career ended by a knee injury, but my real heroes were Messer and Mead. Mead used to walk his dog across Prospect Park and to gain a smile from him as he passed was joy indeed.

It was the usual practice for any youngster arriving a little late at Elm Park and finding that his position in the crowd was way behind the adults, to be lifted and passed over the gown-ups until he was in the front of the crowd against the iron railings.

We all enjoyed our football and there was not a breath of rowdyism or the slightest danger for unaccompanied eight year olds. The only peril I suffered was on one occasion at the end of one of the big matches, when I did not wait for the major part of the crowd to disperse and made my exit into Norfolk Road, wedged in the crowd funnelling through the gate and my feet did not touch the ground for about 10 yards.

Sometimes we had a bonus before the match, Reading Boys would play, (so often it appeared to me) a needle match against Swindon Boys. It was very cheap but splendid entertainment. Memories of happenings at Elm Road throughout Reading Football Club's history are well recorded in *Biscuits & Royals* by David Downs and so I will merely say 'Come on the Biscuitmen!' or bring the cheer up to date with 'Up the Royals!'

Of course, I always hoped to play for Reading one day, but I settled eventually for playing for a team giving Reading Boys a practice match before they had a match at Elm Park. Real fame!.

Reading Football Club on a river outing in the 1930s. Mr Armitage, the chairman is on the right, wearing a bowler hat. Also aboard are the manager Joe Smith, players Palethorpe, Barley, Richie, Eaton, Harston and Bacon, together with trainers Glancy and Lenny, and the groundsman Bart.

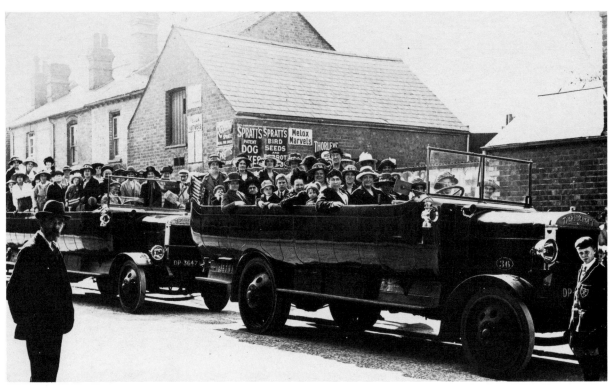

An Elm Park Hall Women's Outing.

Hey-days and Holidays

Holidays for youngsters of Reading in the twenties really meant exciting happenings for them on Bank Holidays, a change from the routine rather than a visit very far away from Reading. Occasionally, for the fortunate ones, a week by the sea-side started. A few days before the holiday the Great Western Railway horse and cart would arrive at one's home to take away a trunk for transit to its holiday destination. This was 'Luggage in Advance' and cost 2/- for a ticket holder. 'Rich people' went to Hayling Island frequently. I had a friend whose father owned a car, a bull-nosed Morris and in about 1924, my friend and I travelled gently to Hayling Island, starting very early in the morning. We sat in the dickey seat and held out our handkerchiefs in the wind and wrote down car numbers in a book, getting the first one as we approached Petersfield.But this was something special. Holidays and hey-days were usually spent closer to home. Bank holidays were often celebrated with a bus ride and picnic in fine weather. I remember going to Burghfield Common, alighting at the Three Firs on the corner of the road leading to the A.W.R.E. at Aldermaston, for a picnic and romp about on the common. The crowded bus which took us could not reach the top of Burghfield Hill, so some of us had to get off the bus, walk up the hill and then wait while the driver went for water to cool the radiator which was gushing steam and boiling water. Bucklebury Common was also a Bank Holiday resort. I remember that I had the idea that wayfarers had a right to call at a public house and request refreshment at any time and consequently, I requested a glass of water from a publican in Bucklebury in mid-afternoon and received one promptly.

Easter was primrose and bluebell time and we youngsters walked regularly to the 'City' in Tilehurst (rather a vague area of woods and dells) to gather flowers, climb trees and set up 'homes' in which to drink our bottle of water and to eat our broken biscuits. Later in the year we would visit Tilehurst again to gather 'moon daisies'. The August Bank holiday was sometimes the time for a little railway journey, chugging up to Pangbourne or to Maidenhead. There were also day excursions to the sea; I recall it was 3/6 return from the old Southern Railway Station (adjacent to the present station) to Littlehampton. But

Christmas of course was the day of days! The excitement and anticipation was unbearable and yet I doubt if I had, before the age of ten, a Christmas present which cost more than 2/6 (12½p). A second-hand Meccano set was my pride and joy and the regular box of 'tuppenny fancies', luxury sweets for those days, mainly chocolate covered marsh-mallows. Some years we had chicken and one bottle of ruby wine; more often I had a bottle of Matthews' Vimto. (1d and 1d on the bottle).

Pleasure came throughout the year in simple ways, regularly and often free. Dr. Hurry had a superb garden at the corner of Southcote Road and Bath Road, full of plants collected from all over the world. The garden was opened to the public in aid of a charity once a year and seeing his exotic plants filled me with the thrill of far off lands and the mystery of the East. Looking back, one is conscious of the difference television has made to one's awareness of the world. Our geography text-books at school were not very helpful either. My Gill's *Geography of the World* dated 1926, has no pictures, only lists of names for learning by heart. In the same way, the Wembley

The approach to Reading Station with the board 'Great Western Railway' across the front of the building, just below the clock tower. Families fortunate enough to take a proper holiday could send their trunk in advance for just two shillings.

On Wings of Song starring Grace Moor was showing at the Pavilion when this photograph was taken.

Exhibition of 1924-27 opened up a new concept of the lands of the British Empire. I visited the exhibition once; we did not spend any money in the fun-fair or in watching the rodeo in Wembley Stadium, we just looked. After nearly sixty years I can still recall the awe and wonder I experienced gazing at the splendours of India, the richness of Africa and the beauty of the tropical islands. But joy was provided by lesser events, the massed bands on Hospital Sunday and the church parade of the Royal Berkshire Regiment being led by its band from Brock Barracks to St. Mary's Church in the Butts. A friend told me that his most vivid memory of this event was the gold lettering on the prayer books glinting in the sun as the marching soldiers swung them in their hands. Listening to the Reading Temperance Band in the Forbury Gardens on a Sunday evening was a big event.

In the twenties I visited the cinema infrequently but my tastes were limited - Charlie Chaplin, Buster Keaton, Harold Lloyd, Douglas Fairbanks and of course Jackie Coogan. Thumbs down for Rudolph Valentino! I saw my first 'talkie' in about 1929 at the 'Pavilion' on the corner of Russell Street; the film was 'Sonny Boy' and I disliked it intensely, thinking it must be the end of all the wonderful films I had seen. I had so enjoyed the films at the Empire in Elm Park Road. The front rows were 3d. for children I believe I paid 4d. (1½p) to watch a great variety of adventure and comedy. But most memorable for me were the frightening serials such as those about Dr. Fu Manchu, torturing his victims in a cage of starving rats. This is the only cinema I have known in which the manager stopped the show and addressed the audience in front of the screen telling it that the performance would not continue unless the cheering ceased. The present day fire officers would thoroughly disapprove of the interval crush as we all surged out to the tuck-shop and loos. Occasionally I went to the Palace in Cheapside 'early doors' to see the music hall stars, but visits to the County Theatre in Friar Street were even more special. My memories of this theatre are solely of the Reading Operatic Society, Gilbert & Sullivan and in particular, Teddy Langston whose humorous interpretations appealed to me.

Huntley & Palmers' athletic meetings and flower shows in the cricket ground in Kensington

Road were grand occasions in the twenties. What a hotch-potch of memories! There was the local soldiery displaying the skill of tent-pegging; the dishes of cooked potatoes in the show, many of them turning an uninviting black; the piglet in the crate at the side of the bowling for the pig alley; the tilting the bucket, an entertaining competition for two in which one propelled a wheelbarrow which held the other one who had to tilt with a pole at a contraption which emptied water over the competitors who were too slow; the frequent falls by racing cyclists on the flat grassy circular track; the deep brown eggs in the show; the magnificent cups and trophies and of course, the roundabouts, the swings, the flowers, the vegetables and finally, the dob of ice-cream on a H. & P's Osborne biscuit.

Sporting events in Palmers Park were more serious and I had the impression as a youngster that here I was seeing the real athletes - world beaters, one day. Even the cattle market in Great Knollys Street was a source of entertainment and nearby came the Fair where my recollections are mainly of mud, looking, but never spending. I cannot believe it was a very lucrative activity for the fair people.

For me, November 5th was fun but most fun was gained by spending my ½d's on fireworks after proper deliberation at Honey's the newsagents in Oxford Road, and then sorting them and enjoying them. They did not take long to let off! There was some local excitement about the bonfire at St. Andrew's Boys' Home in Wilton Road; it was said it contained a tar-barrel and the bonfire was well worth watching from an upstairs window.

Birthday parties brought enjoyment - much enjoyed in the park, the garden and around a loaded table. A game I recall was flower pot racing. Walking on the pots by moving one forward and temporarily balancing on the other. Is there a modern version of this? I was a programme seller at an Agricultural Show in Prospect Park. I don't remember much about it, except for having my tea in a marquee with policemen; I was amazed by the size and appetites of these men. I was a scout at this time and I was looking forward to going to my first camp. I had for some time envied Miss Hopgood's guides setting off for camp from West Reading.

Mr Stanley King (left) outside the old Pavilion cinema in Oxford Road.

The White Hart at Sonning in the 1920s. The notice reads 'Landing Stage for launches of any draught'. Reading folk used to walk to this spot on a summer evening, but only the very few could afford any refreshment here.

There was that occasion when a young friend showed me his home made wireless and fiddled about with the cat's whisker, and through the earphones came forth an often interrupted cacophony of sound. I found it an exhilarating experience but had not the least conception of what it was beginning. In fact, an awful lot has happened between the 1920s and the 1980s!

As children we played all manner of games in the street. What pleasure we obtained from cigarette cards! Collecting sets was the result of a great deal of swapping - sets of Dickens' characters, cartoons of Famous People, Cars, Film Stars, Military Badges, Breeds of Dogs, Farm Animals, Trees, etc., etc. Some of the title cards were too complicated for us and so we simplified them; for example, 'Strugglers' were 'Plants which struggle for existence'. We played 'gambling' games with our spares. We flicked them to knock down other cards propped up against a step or alternatively to partially cover those already flicked. There was some skill in flicking a fag-card well.

I suppose we were not so health conscious in the twenties and that is why we often played marbles in the gutter, stuffing our winnings into our pockets. No wonder we had dirty handkerchiefs! Mostly we played with cheap 'clays' and only one special glass alley was needed for our games. We were very sexist; girls never played marbles but indulged instead in individual skipping or communal skipping accompanied by traditional rhymes. Boys never skipped! But we all had our hoops; boys mostly had iron ones with a metal hook to control them and there were also wooden ones, propelled by a rounded wooden stick. Hop-scotch pitches were chalked on most of the side street pavements and the rules of this game were well established. Then there was the season of tops. Whipping or spinning tops were a halfpenny each; there were the easier to manage slower solid ones and the racy T-shaped ones. Having coloured the surface with our crayons and made ourselves a whip from a stick and a piece of string, we would whip away merrily for hours on the pavement outside of our homes, only stopping at times to renew or vary the pattern of our top. Again, skill was needed to keep the top spinning and even more to make it hop through the air without stopping to spin.

Five-stones was played but not with the present day manufactured 'five-stone' but with five real stones carefully selected for equality of size and shape.

Scooters were a luxury! I enjoyed scooting around the streets, wearing out one boot sole more than the other. My scooter was a simple wooden one (some were all metal) but I could reach a good speed and apart from the intense enjoyment it gave me, it was useful for reaching friends in the next street in quick time.

Most frequently, we resorted to playing with a ball. We were adept at throwing it at a wall and catching it with all kinds of intervening clapping and leg movements. Sometimes we had to be content with bouncing it to the accompaniment of rhymes and variations of bounces.

Did any of us complain that we were bored and didn't know what to do? I don't think so.

'Midweek' readers have reminded me of all kinds of simple happenings that brought us joy in our childhood, but I think the first prize must go to Calvert & Yilley's in St. Mary's Butts. The excitement of young girls being bought items of clothing there has lasted sixty years or more. Other feel like Joan Martin of Tilehurst. She was indeed a princess on Sundays in her straw hat with shiny red cherries on the side, worn with a white broderie anglais dress with a large blue ribbon sash at the waist.

The Palace theatre was obviously a great favourite of families in the twenties and many, including W. Peedell of Mortimer Common, remember queueing along the draughty side of this music-hall for seats in the Gods (the gallery) 5d. early doors and 4d. when the best seats had gone.

Two ex call boys at the Palace Theatre, T.C. Dac Higgins and Mr. Kirby, Whitley Wood can recall Gracie Fields in 'Mrs. Tower of London' and the chorus girls getting 30 shillings per week. I have also been reminded that the famous Bertram Mills Circus used to pitch the tent behind Vincents Motor Show rooms near the station and this created excitement for even those who could not afford to attend.

The father of P.R. Middleton of Tilehurst used

to assert that the only paid holiday he got was the 2 minutes silence on 11th November each year. This occasion was something special. During the twenties this celebration of the end of the 1914-18 War at the 11th hour of the 11th day of the 11th month brought not only pedestrians, but all traffic to a halt for 2 minutes. It was most impressive and I never knew of anyone breaking the silence. I believe there was real and honest remembrance of this terrible time.

There are claims that both Elm Park Road Cinema and the Caversham Electric was the Twopenny Plunge. Perhaps they were both called this. Anyway we all enjoyed visiting these 'flea-pits' and it has been suggested that it was all part of our education.

I am told that Pitch and Toss was played at the bottom of George Street on Sundays, and my age group were used to keep a look out for the police and earned a few coppers for being ready to shout 'Skib-O!'

As youngsters, most of us were tucked up in bed on New Year's Eve and took no part in any celebrations, but occasionally waking to hear the factory hooters and the G.W.R. engines' whistles and the few neighbours exchanging greetings in the streets. 'Happy New Year!' they would call and then start worrying about where tomorrow's meal was coming from.

Reading Town Hall looking rather splendid in the twenties. The **Reading Chronicle** *offices are now on the right of the picture and the entrance to the original Arcade can be seen in the background. In the foreground evidence for the need for 'dung boys' can clearly be seen.*

Fleeting Memories

I am still relying upon memory and not resorting to doing any research; it is surprising how the memories return after sixty years and once embarked upon this task, like Topsy they grow and grow.

The General Strike in 1926 presented a strange excitement to me. I had the idea that something extraordinary was happening. Witnessing the gaunt miners marching through Reading disturbed me. My grandfather who worked hard until he was worn out at seventy-two, explained to me that some people did not know their station in life or the way that things were supposed to be. At the same time, a young pal told me proudly that his dad, a printer was on strike and that printers and tram-drivers were the only workers in Reading to support the miners and the railway men. It was all rather confusing for a young lad, but at the end of the strike I had a feeling of sadness which I barely understood.

Poverty, *real* poverty was there for all to see in Reading in the twenties. Not all children had footwear and I have seen children going to school around 1922 with newspaper tied around their feet. For many, a penny a week assured care at the Royal Berkshire Hospital and another penny a week gained medicines from the Reading Dispensary in Chain Street. It was sad lot, too, for the 'dung boys', very young boys, not long passed fourteen, who kept the streets cleared of horse manure. In spite of their smart uniform and colourful hand-carts, they were not regarded highly. In fact, it was a useful insult to call after an adversary, 'You'll be a dung boy when you grow up!'

Life was generally more uncomfortable sixty years ago. All of the many terraced houses of Reading had no bathrooms and the choice of a place to wash was between the unlit scullery and at the wash-stand with china wash basin and jug in the freezing cold, candle-lit bedrooms with frost covered sash cord windows. Gas lit the streets and gas lit most houses. The gas light with its fragile mantle would be usually up in one corner of the room, so that the man of the family could read his paper more easily than the women, sitting elsewhere could see to do their mending. Most gas in Reading was paid for by putting pennies in the meter and the day the gas man called to empty the meter, there were smiles abroad, for there were a few pence to come as rebate.

A particular nuisance to me as a boy was my bicycle lamp, even more irritating than my rear reflector which frequently fell off. I often cycled from one side of the Oxford Road to the other in order to consult a school mate about some home-work difficulties. My cheap paraffin lamp either blew out or gave off thick smoke, making me extremely dirty. I envied those with acetylene lamps. Cycles were dense along the main roads in Reading, soon after the hooters sounded from the factories at the end of the working day. In the twenties, there were times when it was nigh impossible to cross the road around the biscuit factory because of the rush of bicycles homeward bound, and Kings Road and Oxford Road were only a little less difficult to cross. However, bicycles enabled us to get around and could be hired for 6d. an hour. I remember that there were at least two shops in the side streets in Reading, one of them, Hamilton's, where an ancient grandad had this separate business from the yard of the little shop. I went always on my bike to the swimming baths, at first, to the Tilehurst Road baths on the southern side of the road between the ends of Connaught Road and Belmont Road. This was the coldest, and most unpleasant swimming area I have ever experienced. Naturally, no mixed public bathing in the twenties and it seems that the designers of swimming baths went beyond reason in order to acquire privacy. Tilehurst Road baths were entirely enclosed and the glass canopy was of deep green glass, ensuring that no sunlight ever warmed the interior. All paintwork was green and every word one spoke had a hollow echo. Rarely were there many bathers there, which was not surprising, as it was so cold and it's hard to believe that anyone ever enjoyed learning to swim there. There was King's Meadows' Swimming bath too, mainly open air and for males only, but females had their own anti-peeping tom building. Both were close to Reading lock. The water was straight from the river and I taught myself to swim here, frequently slipping on the slimy bottom of the baths and in company with minnows and dace. What a joy it was to experience the comforts of King's Road baths in later years! Coley swimming bath was similar to the one at King's Meadow, but would you believe it? We could be seen three

hundred yards away from the bridge in Berkeley Avenue.

One of the sights of Reading in 1923 was the completion of the building of a replacement for the old Reading Bridge. The strength and success of the new bridge was tested by having dozens of steam-rollers go across it at one time, before it was officially opened. As a young lad, I waited for them all to collapse into the river. How absurd it was! I wonder what would have happened if the event had finished by proving the bridge was unsafe and a catastrophe. Caversham Bridge was completed in 1926 and we were all looking forward to it being opened by the Prince of Wales, but the ceremony was cancelled owing to the impact of the General Strike.

Before 1926, someone gave me an old *Dunlop Motoring Guide*. It in were advertised a Clyno car at £145 and a super 10 hp Gwynne Saloon at £285. Chauffeurs were employed widely and smart hats for them were advertised at 12/6 (62½p). That reminds me that we all wore hats in those days; I remember Elm Park being a sea of caps and trilbies. Also in the motoring guide, the Grand Hotel in Blagrave Street was

A Corporation bus of 1927. In the inter-war years, however, most men got to work by bicycle, and the roads near factories would be dense with swarms of men pedalling home when the hooter sounded the end of their working day.

offering 'R. & B. for 8/-' (40p) and the Ship Hotel in Duke Street offered 'R.B. & A. for 8/6' (42½p). It appears that 'Attention', whatever that was, cost 2½p! The George has a great advantage over all the others, announcing 'Fitted throughout with electric light'.

Not far along Oxford Road, roughly opposite where the Ramada Hotel now stands, was Jackson's, wholesalers of rags and bones and nearly every other discarded item, and where all the barrow loads of the lesser rag and bone merchants ended. It was a busy, dirty, smelly hole and would have made a good set for the slum scene in a film, but at least it was on the side of 'Waste not, want not' - conservation we call it now. There was not much we could not take, when we were hard up, to Jacksons and exchange for a few pence. Most of the children of the twenties had experience of selling old newspapers, jam-jars, worn out clothes and well boiled bones to Jackson's. Nearly opposite was Warwicks the timber merchants who had a large yard, and timber was produced from tree trunks right in the centre of town. Sawdust could be bought there cheaply and customers could see dangerous unguarded circular saws. Legislation about safety was sorely needed. Nearby in Hosier Street was another Warwicks, manufacturers of bicycles, particularly of errand boys' cycles, very sturdy and heavy, with a rack in front to hold a basket; they also produce three wheelers, slow and hard work to propel, with the front body for carrying the goods.

Watt's the cycle shop opposite McIlroys, had a part of an aircraft in the side entrance. Apparently we all had inaccurate but exciting ideas of the source of this relic, but most agreed it was part of the plane that Colonel Cody flew at Farnborough and in which he was killed.

I wrote earlier of 'dung boys'. It was reassuring to learn that many of them did well. Geoff Tomlin of Curzon Street gives much of the credit for the efficiency and industry of these boys to the foreman, Jack Halliday who marched the street orderlies to work in military fashion, insisted things being done correctly but at the same time protected his boys as if they were his sons. Mr. Stratton says he was well paid in this job - 16/3 per week in 1929; he enjoyed over-time when elephants appeared at the Palace Theatre and were exercised around town.

Apart from the silent films at the Vaudeville Cinema in Broad Street we all marvelled at the changing coloured lights focused on the screen, and of course Edward Parlovitz was for most of us, the only conductor of an orchestra we had ever seen. So quite rightly, we held him in great esteem. Anyone having piano lessons in Queen Victoria Street at his studio with the great man was also respected.

My dancing days were not in the twenties, but I imagine from reading of my correspondents' enthusiasm for happy evenings spent in Reading's dance-halls, that 1920s dances were much the same as those in the 1930s. There were not many private enterprise dances, most of these functions were organised by firms and clubs. The Heelas dance, the Wellsteeds' dance, Huntley & Palmers' Social Club dance, the Old Blues' dance, Boots' dance were just a few. The bands were local and of a good standard and we confined the dances to the quick-step, fox-trot and waltz. Everything was very proper. We asked girls politely if they would like to dance and after the dance returned them to their table and thanked them. Mostly we were in small parties.

The favourite dance halls were the Palm Lodge in West Street, the Central Ballroom, part of the cinema building in Friar Street, Olympia in London Street, the Oxford just off the Oxford Road, the Majestic Ballroom in Caversham Road and the Grosvenor in Caversham. Many started in a simpler way in one of the many Reading Church Halls which had a weekly 'hop' mostly for learners. How nerve-racking it was to hold a girl in one's arms for the very first time!

Just a few more brief memories - Phippens' Nurseries in Oxford Road, near George Street and Lees' Nurseries in Connaught Road; brick kilns and clay-pits all around Water Road; shunting goods' wagons under the bridge in Berkeley Avenue and west of Reading Station clanging and clashing all night long; Huntley, Bourne & Stevens' biscuit tin making factory in London Street and Southampton Street; Charles Powis, partner in a Reading cycle firm, buying land in about 1928 for an airfield which eventually became Woodley Aerodrome; the hand-carts which the police used to take away the drunks from central Reading, especially on Saturday night. (For some time I was convinced these were dead bodies!) What a host of memories return! But I wonder if the older readers are like me and ask 'What was the name of the lady we met, yesterday, dear?'

The Abbey ruins adjacent to the Forbury Gardens, nearly overwhelmed by ivy in the 1920s. It was a splendid site for games of hide and seek in spite of the sinister walls of the nearby Reading Prison.

Childhood Wanderings

In the twenties, I am sure that children remained longer within the family and the family's activities for most of their school-days. Even so, in common with most Reading children, I was allowed to wander and find my own pleasure, invent pastimes for myself, using imagination and whatever nature provided. This enjoyment was all free. I doubt if I ever went out with friends up to the age of ten with more than a penny in my pocket. My wanderings around Reading, however, gave me riches which have lasted all my life.

Prospect Park was my usual destination for early wanderings but there were interesting deviations. There was the short cut from Norfolk Road to Tilehurst Road through 'The Pit' behind Elm Park, which was a steep sided, dangerous piece of waste-ground, which nowadays would not be left for all and sundry to risk breaking their necks. It was a perfect place for war games and the rusty old pieces of corrugated iron were ideal for sliding down the slopes of the pit. It was an adventure playground though also a source of cuts, bruises and dirty clothes. The other early discovery was also a pit; the one on the other side of the Bath Road, near Circuit Lane, reached by the tunnel under the road from the park, reputedly once the hiding place of Dick Turpin. There was water at the bottom of this pit that was foul and unpleasant but it provided the setting for big game hunting and escapes from prowling mammoths and monsters. At this time, there was no development south of the A4. Crossing it led to my childhood playground and the road was safe for youngsters to cross; horse and motor traffic were then in equal quantities. The sight to be stared at was the Greyhound coach, steadily making its way from London to Bristol and later superseded by Thackeray's red coaches. Southcote Lane and Circuit Lane were then country lanes leading to footpaths and farmland and to the other side of the railway lines on which the Cornish Riviera Express (G.W.R) steamed and sent plumes of smoke and steam across the marsh-lands. This area around the Kennet and the canal abounded with yellow irises, marsh buttercups, the great water plantain, ragged robins, cotton-sedge, horse tails, lady's smock and several kinds of orchid. We called this area the Wire-mills. The cattle took little notice of us and we appreciated the small bays they had created for their drinking places. In these, we paddled and began the races of our boats of paper, match-box, leaf and flower head. We climbed trees, set up 'camp', stalked wild creatures, collected flowers for pressing and mounting, bird's-nested, ate our picnic and drank our bottle of water, jumped, rolled, heaved and pulled. What an appetite we had on returning home; bread and jam never tasted as wonderful since that time.

There were variations for reaching this haven. It made a change to reach it by skirting Coley Park or by Calcot Mill where the footpath was marshalled by a playful horse which made it necessary to find a detour. There was also a lane three hundred yards or so along the Burghfield Road, leading to Circuit Lane. Here was a large farm house where I earned from the farmer's wife an egg for tea, for standing my ground bravely when a barking, snarling dog had actually petrified me. We often wandered farther still towards Burghfield and the journey home was made frequently in a state of exhaustion. Cheekily, we once called in The Cunning Man, then the pub on the opposite side of the road to the present one and asked for a glass of water. The

90

Buckets crossing Grovelands Road to Collier's Kiln carrying clay for the making of bricks. Flats stand on the corner today.

The Forbury Gardens in its heyday in the twenties. The beautifully tended flower beds were regarded as a show piece for Sutton's seeds. On Sundays a quiet, neatly dressed group of people would gather round the bandstand to listen to the Reading Temperance Band. On week-days the peace was disturbed by the clangs of colliding goods trucks in the Southern Railway Marshalling Yards between the Gardens and King's Meadows.

two ladies who kept the pub invited us in and gave us each a slice of cold Christmas pudding. I believe that it was customary for them to serve their normal patrons similarly.

Cockney Hill, a lonely lane, was another direction in which to wander and on the right, ascending the hill, was a wood where we worked out our fantasies. We might not have ever entered these woods, but the notice, 'Trespassers will be Prosecuted', was a challenge not to be ignored. Tilehurst, a village then unconnected to Reading was actually reached by a footpath across the allotments behind The Pulsometer in Oxford Road. This was known as the Golf Links, but I have to admit that for many years I though it was called the 'Goal Flinks'. Collecting primroses, bluebells and moon-daisies was sometimes the reason for going to what we called the City. Tilehurst could also be reached in our rambles by going around what is now the Calcot Golf Club but was then the estate of Sir Felix Pole, the Chairman of the Great Western Railway Co. There were ways into this park but only for a little distance, just to see how close we could get to the herd of deer. Between Horncastle and the George & Dragon there was a hazel plantation, grown commercially, and as the owner's son was a school friend, I was fortunate to have another area of exploration.

Water Road was the centre of the brick making industry and buckets travelling on cables brought clay to the kilns. Around the site were a number of paths (one was Lover's Lane) and in all directions there were disused pits, filled with water and littered with bits and pieces, including old planks. We made slippery rafts and sailed forth. A most dangerous game but we suffered only when we returned home, with our clothes covered in clay. There were splendid 'sailing clubs' between Water Road and Waverley Road.

We wandered to the other ends of Reading at times. Reading lock and the adjacent playing fields were places where there was always activity. Apart from the comings and goings to the King's Meadows swimming baths (men's and women's separate), there was help needed by the lock-keeper to push open the lock gates. The nearby Clappers were exciting for their own sake with their rushing water, noise and foam, but disturbing because it was here that Mrs. Dyer, the murderess had stood and thrown babies into the water. We only threw stones. The opening of the Solly Joel's playing field provided the incentive for another expedition. The free roundabouts and swings there gave us a new experience; this activity was so unusual that I suffered giddiness and worse at my first visit. We explored the Warren, Whiteknights, The Holy Brook, the Dreadnought, the Forbury Gardens and the Abbey Ruins, and most places outside Reading's limits; The Three Tunns, Whitley Pump, the Pond House, the two bridges and Prospect Park. I knew Reading well! Young people today seem to gain emotional experience and excitement second hand from the T.V. I had mine for real.

The Millhouse.